THE CIVIL WAR

LOST CAUSE

The End of the Civil War, 1864-1865

James R. Arnold and Roberta Wiener

LERNER PUBLICATIONS COMPANY • MINNEAPOLIS

**First American edition published in 2002
by Lerner Publications Company**

Copyright © 2002 by Lerner Publications Company

The Civil War series is created and produced by Graham Beehag Books,
in cooperation with Lerner Publications Company, a division of
Lerner Publishing Group.

Lerner Publications Company
A division of Lerner Publishing Group
241 First Avenue North
Minneapolis, Minnesota 55401 U.S.A.

Website address: www.lernerbooks.com

Library of Congress Cataloging-in-Publication Data

Arnold, James R.
   Lost cause : the end of the Civil War, 1864-1865 / by James R. Arnold
and Roberta Wiener.
      p. cm.—(The Civil War)
   Includes bibliographical references and index.
   ISBN 0-8225-2317-5 (lib. bdg.)
   1. United States—History—Civil War, 1861–1865—Campaigns—
Juvenile literature. 2. Atlanta Campaign, 1864—Juvenile literature.
3. Appomattox Campaign, 1865—Juvenile literature.
I. Wiener, Roberta, 1952– II. Title.
   E470 .A73   2002
   973.7'3—dc21   2001002224

Printed in Singapore
Bound in the United States of America
1 2 3 4 5 6 – OS – 07 06 05 04 03 02

The authors are grateful to Katy Holmgren, whose excellent editing of
the manuscript has made this book such a pleasure to read.

*Front cover picture: A painting of Grant accepting Lee's surrender at
Appomattox. The artist chose to depict the two leaders in clean uniforms
at the same table. In reality, they sat at separate tables, and Grant,
spattered with mud, came directly from the field.*

Back cover picture: The burning of Columbia, South Carolina, February 1865

CONTENTS

WORDS YOU NEED TO KNOW

base: a place where an army or navy keeps its food and supplies

blockade: warships organized to keep all ships from delivering goods and supplies to an enemy harbor. During the Civil War, the North set up blockades of all Southern ports.

breastworks: wood and dirt that have been piled up to protect soldiers

campaign: a series of military actions, such as marches and battles, to capture a certain place

cavalry: a group of soldiers who move and fight on horseback

command: the position of being in charge of soldiers

defenses: a line of fieldworks and forts around an area, such as a town, that an army is trying to protect

fieldworks: trenches and breastworks to protect soldiers on a battlefield

flank: one side of a group of soldiers

monitor: a type of navy ship covered with iron armor

morale: the confidence, courage, and fighting spirit of soldiers

rally: to reorganize and encourage frightened soldiers

reinforce: to send soldiers into a battle, after it has begun, to help their side win

rout: to run away in panic

veteran: an experienced soldier who has fought in battles

INTRODUCTION
HOPING FOR VICTORY

The victory of Union general Ulysses S. Grant at Chattanooga, Tennessee, was the last important Civil War battle of 1863. Chattanooga followed the siege of Vicksburg and the Battle of Gettysburg, which were both Union victories. After more than two and a half long years of war, these victories gave Northern people hope that the Civil War would soon end in victory for the Union. Some Southern people began to lose hope. But most still believed that their cause was just and that their God would grant them victory if they kept fighting. In Virginia, soldiers believed their great general, Robert E. Lee, would lead them to victory.

In the spring of 1864, a New York soldier wrote to his father from his camp in Virginia, "Well, we are making preparations for the coming contest, which . . . cannot be postponed much longer." After a long winter in camp, he was ready for a fight. "The sooner we get at it the better."

CHAPTER ONE

The Campaign of 1864

The winter of 1863–1864 was the hardest yet for Southern soldiers. Many did not have enough to eat. A Georgia soldier named Milton Barrett wrote that all he got to eat each day was two-thirds of a pound of flour and one-third of a pound of bacon. He used this to make "cush"—a mix of moldy corn bread and pork grease. Cush hardly kept a man alive. Men had little choice but to try to steal food. Milton Barrett was a fine soldier. Yet he wrote about stealing, "Hunger will cause a man to do almost anything."

Hunger, discouragement about the war, and worry about their families caused some soldiers to desert the army. Although deserters were executed, more and more rebels tried to leave the army and go home. A Virginia soldier wrote in his diary on January 8, 1864, "Saw a man shot today for desertion. Poor fellow! His crime was only going home to see after his wife and children. It was his third or fourth [time]. His name was Martin. He was buried where he was executed. Did he not die for his country?"

In July 1863, Union general Ulysses S. Grant's successful siege of Vicksburg had gained the Union control of shipping on the Mississippi River. Union control of the Mississippi River divided the Confederacy in two. The Union navy's blockade of Southern ports kept foreign trading ships from bringing supplies to the South. Confederate soldiers and civilians suffered from shortages of weapons, clothing, and tools for the war.

The Confederate railroad system had been used mostly to carry cotton from the countryside to

Soldiers rest in a field hospital.

the ports. The system had always been small, with few trains and few miles of track. During the Civil War, the army used the railroad to carry food and supplies. Gradually, machine parts wore out and couldn't be replaced—the parts were made only in the North. The trains broke down. The food grown east of the Mississippi River could not move to the armies. The Union capture of Vicksburg also kept cattle and corn from the Confederate states west of the Mississippi from reaching the hungry people in the east.

DESERTERS

Before the Civil War, many soldiers had been poor farmers. When they went to war, their wives had to do all of the farmwork. Soldiers worried about how their families could get enough to eat. Union and Confederate soldiers also grew tired and discouraged as the war went on. Their lives were hard and dangerous. Many questioned whether their cause was worth leaving home and risking their lives. Some soldiers received worrying letters from home about how hard things were. All of these things led soldiers to desert their armies.

About 200,000 Union soldiers and about 100,000 Confederate soldiers deserted during the Civil War—about one soldier in ten on each side. The number of Union desertions climbed to its highest point— several hundred each day—during the cold, wet winter of 1862–1863. A discouraged Union soldier wrote to his sister two days before Christmas 1862, "I have nothing cheerful to write. Although I am well and able to do duty, I am very unhappy." Like most soldiers, he was willing to put up with a hard life, "if it is to do any good, but every thing looks dark, not

The Union and the Confederacy both executed deserters (soldiers who leave the army before their tour of duty is over). This illustration shows a Union deserter who has been shot by a firing squad. Like other deserters, he was forced to sit on the coffin in which he would later be buried.

because the [S]outh [is] strong but because our leaders are [bad.]" This unhappy soldier concluded, "The whole thing is rotten to the core." Another Union soldier wrote home that "the men [are] all dying off pretty fast . . . I am lonesome and down hearted. . . . I am tired of Blood Shed and have Saw Enough of it."

On the Southern side, more and more Confederates deserted as the war went on. Desertions increased with each passing year as Southern soldiers

sensed that the South was losing the war. When deserters were caught, they were punished. If a soldier had a good record, he might receive light punishment, such as loss of pay or extra guard duty. Many Confederate officers were so desperate for soldiers near the end of the war that they would take deserters back into the army without punishing them. Some officers on each side handed out harsher punishments. They whipped or branded (burned with hot irons) deserters. Officers could send them to prison for up to five years. Some deserters were hanged or shot by a firing squad.

A Confederate soldier deserted after his starving wife wrote him, "before God, Edward, unless you come home we must die." Edward was caught by Confederate patrols and tried for desertion. He showed this letter at his trial but was sentenced to death anyway. Fortunately for the soldier and his family, General Robert E. Lee heard of the case and ordered the man's life to be spared.

In January 1863, a Pennsylvania soldier wrote, "Dear Folks at Home: Today I witnessed what I never did before, the drumming out of a deserter. . . . The prisoner was called out, his head shaven, the iron heated, pants turned down and brand applied, the army buttons cut off his clothes—a squad of soldiers with fixed bayonets placed behind him when the band struck up the rogues' march."

Generals thought that the threat of being shot by a firing squad would keep soldiers from deserting. In order to make this threat real, generals sometimes ordered deserters shot. First, thousands of soldiers, like the Pennsylvania soldier described above, marched to the scene of the execution. They formed a hollow square so that all had a clear view. The deserter was blindfolded and made to kneel by an open grave or to sit or stand on a coffin.

The viewers fell silent. The firing squad approached. A soldier called, "Fire!" The squad shot their muskets. The soldiers marched by to see the dead deserter. It was awful, and no one liked it. An Alabama soldier saw an execution. He wrote, "I saw a sight today that made me feel mighty Bad. I saw a man shot for deserting. . . . Martha it was one sight that I did hate to see."

Soldiers knew that the folks back home were suffering too. But in spite of the South's important losses, many people still thought that the South could win the war. A Confederate doctor toured the South. He got a sense of the people's spirit and wrote, "Our Virginia people are as determined as ever, and hopeful." Tens of thousands of Confederate soldiers stayed in the army. Even if they had lost hope that they could win, they were too stubborn to give up.

Confederate president Jefferson Davis was the most stubborn of all. Davis knew American history. He knew that during the American Revolution (1775–1783) there had been times when it seemed like the war was lost. George Washington had stubbornly kept fighting for American independence. Davis was determined to do the same for Southern independence.

Even so, Davis knew that the South's best chance was for Abraham Lincoln to lose the next presidential election in the North, which would take place in November 1864. If enough people in the North were tired of the war, they would vote for a candidate who promised to stop the war.

President Lincoln understood that he would have a better chance of getting reelected if the North won an important battle before the elections. Then people who were tired of the war would believe that the North would soon win. Lincoln hoped Grant could give him this victory.

Lincoln promoted Grant to lieutenant general, the highest rank in the army. Grant was the first officer to hold this rank since George Washington.

Confederate president Jefferson Davis hoped that a rebel victory in battle would make Lincoln lose the election. Davis's generals understood this. One wrote that if the Confederates could "throw back" the Union forces, Lincoln "will not be able to recover his position . . . until the Presidential election is over, and we shall then have a new President to treat with. If Lincoln has any success early he will be able to get more men and may be able to . . . [win] reelection."

11

General Grant, seated, did not frighten the rebels. One later wrote, "We wanted Grant [to meet] General Lee and the Army of Northern Virginia, and to let him have a smell of our powder. For we knew we simply could never be driven off a battlefield."

Grant now commanded all U.S. armies—about 533,000 soldiers. Grant traveled to Washington to receive his promotion. He decided to stay in the east to personally supervise the North's most important army, the Army of the Potomac. The winning general at the Battle of Gettysburg, George Meade, stayed in command of the Army of the Potomac. But now he was under Grant's command.

Grant made some important changes in the Army of the Potomac. In the past, thousands of soldiers had stayed in the rear, behind the battle lines. They guarded the railroads and defended Washington, D.C. Grant ordered many of them to rejoin the fighting ranks (soldiers on the battlefield). The veterans (the soldiers who had been fighting in the army for years) liked this decision. They felt that it was high time for the rear area soldiers to share the danger of fighting in a battle.

Grant also reduced the number of wagons carrying supplies so that the army could march faster and the wagon drivers could rejoin the ranks. One Massachusetts soldier was walking past the wagon train when a mule snorted. He looked at the mule and said, "You need not laugh at me, you may be in the ranks yourself before Grant gets through with the army."

Grant had come to the White House in March 1864. Union political leaders and their families were eager to meet him. A group of women asked his wife, Julia Dent Grant, if the general could capture Richmond, Virginia, the Confederate capital. Julia Grant answered, "Yes, before he gets through. Mr. Grant always was a very obstinate [stubborn] man."

Grant's strategy (military plan) for 1864 was simple. In the east, Meade's Army of the Potomac was to attack Lee's Army of Northern Virginia. Grant told Meade, "Wherever Lee goes, there you will go also." In the west, Grant gave command of the most important army to William T. Sherman. Sherman's mission was to defeat the rebel Army of Tennessee. Grant also ordered the smaller Union armies to advance toward the enemy armies. Their jobs were to make sure that the Confederates could not send reinforcements to the main rebel armies. Lincoln strongly approved of Grant's plan to use all the Union armies at once.

Grant called for three separate Union forces to invade Virginia. General Franz Sigel was in

Grant trusted General William T. Sherman, above, to command the Union armies in Georgia.

A unit of Civil War soldiers drills with their cannons.

charge of the Union forces in western Virginia and in Virginia's Shenandoah Valley. His job was to engage rebel forces in the Shenandoah Valley. Meade's Army of the Potomac would attack Lee in central Virginia. Benjamin Butler's Army of the James would move up the James River and destroy an important railroad between the Confederate cities of Petersburg and Richmond. In the west, Sherman would drive on Atlanta, Georgia. Nathaniel Banks's troops would move from Louisiana toward Mobile, Alabama. This move would help Sherman by distracting the rebel Army of Tennessee.

Grant's strategy was sensible, but there were

three major problems. First, Sigel, Butler, and Banks were terrible generals. They had been beaten time and again. Lincoln had given them their jobs because he needed their political support during his campaign for the presidency. The second major problem was the power of an army in a defensive position. Lee's Army of Northern Virginia, defending from sheltered positions, would have a huge advantage over the attackers. The third major problem was the genius of Robert E. Lee. Lee had won almost every battle he fought in Virginia. The spring campaign of 1864 would show whether he could keep winning against the Union army under its new leader.

CHAPTER TWO

The Fighting Begins

As spring approached, the Union Army of the Potomac prepared to advance against the Confederate Army of Northern Virginia. The march would take Grant's army through the Wilderness, an area of thick trees, bushes, and vines and small streams and swamps. Lee had beaten Union general Joseph Hooker there the year before. Lee knew that a Confederate victory in the Wilderness could stop the Union from reaching Richmond. The Union had more men and artillery. But it would be very hard for the Union leaders to use them while moving through the Wilderness. The swampy ground would slow them down, and the woods would make it difficult to aim at and hit the enemy.

The Union army's march began on May 4, 1864. General Winfield Hancock's II Corps, a part of the Army of the Potomac, reached the crossroads at Chancellorsville, Virginia, before 10 A.M. This was good progress. But the Army of the Potomac's huge wagon train of food and supplies moved more slowly. For the rest of the day, Hancock's men waited for the wagons at Chancellorsville.

The Union soldiers looked around the crossroads and saw the grim sights from the Battle of Chancellorsville the year before. One soldier described the scene: "Weather-stained [pieces] of clothing, rusty gun-barrels and bayonets . . . bleaching bones and grinning skulls [covered the ground]."

Drummer boys wake Union soldiers to begin a march.

The slowness of the Union march gave Lee's Army of Northern Virginia a chance to find and attack Grant's army. On a beautiful spring day, May 5, 1864, the Battle of the Wilderness began. Because the fighting took place in the thick woods, no battle line could march and keep in order. Men could see only fifty yards or less. Fighting broke out with little warning. All the officers could see was "smoke and bushes and lots of our men tumbling about." Because of these conditions, the officers could not control their men.

A general told one of Meade's aides, or helpers, that thousands of rebels were only three hundred yards away. The aide looked around and saw no one. He later wrote, "For all I could see, they might have been in Florida."

Lee's army attacked with great spirit. The intense, confused fighting lasted all day. Both sides lost many men. In the past, many army commanders had cracked (gotten scared and given up) from the pressure of fighting against Lee and his army.

Union soldiers in Virginia cross the Rapidan River at Germanna Ford as they march toward the Wilderness.

Grant did not. During the fighting, an anxious Union general rode to Grant. He said that the crisis had come. Lee was about to surround the Army of the Potomac. Grant was normally calm. This report made him angry.

He replied, "Oh, I am heartily tired of hearing about what Lee is going to do. Some of you always seem to think he is suddenly going to turn a double somersault and land in our rear and on both our flanks [sides] at the same time. Go back to your command, and try to think what we are going to do ourselves instead of what Lee is going to do."

Neither side had won by the time night fell, so the battle continued at dawn the next day, May 6. In the morning, the Union attacked. Hancock's corps routed the rebels. The beaten Confederates abandoned their line and fled.

Soon after the rout, General James Longstreet arrived with Confederate reinforcements, including the famous Texas Brigade. Lee shook his hand and said, "I was never so glad to see you. Hancock has broken my line." The two generals rallied (encouraged and reorganized) their men.

General Grant calmly sat on a stump smoking a cigar while the Battle of the Wilderness raged.

Then the Texas Brigade charged the Yankees. Lee rode with them to encourage them. It was not the job of the top general to be in the front line. The Texans knew it. They said that they could beat the Yankees without Lee's help. They loved Lee and told him to move to safety. "Lee to the rear," they cried. "I never heard such a shout," said a Texas major. Lee took off his hat to salute his brave Texans as he left.

The Texans plugged the hole in the Confederate line. They drove back Hancock's men. But they suffered terribly. Union bullets struck more than half the Texans who began the charge.

For the rest of the day, the fighting raged. At one point, the soldiers commanded by Longstreet and Hancock fought to control a line of log breastworks (trees cut down and piled together to make a defense) at a crossroads. Even when the logs caught fire from all the shooting, the men still fought. A Union soldier wrote, "The men fought the enemy and the flames at the same time. Their hair and beards were singed and their faces blistered."

Finally night came, and the battle ended. On May 7, the two exhausted armies rested. That night Grant gave an order for the Army of the

Confederate breastworks, below left, in the Wilderness. These piles of logs and dirt were very difficult to attack because the defenders could take cover behind them and shoot down the attackers.

Potomac to march through the forest. The soldiers feared that it might be another retreat, just like the year before. A Union soldier wrote that the soldiers' feelings about Grant depended "on the direction we turned at the Chancellorsville House. If to the left [a retreat], he was to be rated with Meade and Hooker and Burnside and Pope [the generals who had failed]. . . . [W]e turned to the right [toward Spotsylvania, an advance]. . . . [O]ur spirits rose. We . . . began to sing. . . . That night we were happy." When Grant ordered the army to keep advancing, he made one of the great decisions of the war.

The Battle of the Wilderness was a draw, with heavy losses on both sides. No one ever knew how many men the two armies lost during the battle. Probably the Union had more than 17,000 casualties (men killed, wounded, and missing). The Confederates lost about 7,750 men.

Wounded soldiers from the Battle of the Wilderness, below. Union General John Gibbon observed, "Two things had been pretty well demonstrated by the two days' fight; Lee could not force us from our position and we could not force him from his."

24

CHAPTER THREE

The Bloody Angle and Beyond

Grant's next idea was to move around Lee's right flank to Spotsylvania Court House. Spotsylvania sat at a junction of roads leading to Richmond. It was the next important place on the road from the Wilderness to Richmond.

Even before Grant gave his orders to begin this march, Lee was getting ready to meet him. A Confederate general asked Lee if he had any special reports to suggest what Grant was going to do.

"Not at all," Lee answered. He added, "Spotsylvania is now General Grant's best strategic point. I am so sure of his next move that I have already made arrangements to march by the shortest . . . route, that we may next meet him there." Correctly figuring out where Grant was headed again showed Lee's genius for war.

The Union infantry and artillery marched toward Spotsylvania. Grant had given command of the army's cavalry to General Philip Sheridan. Like Grant, Sheridan had fought in the west. Sheridan's brave conduct impressed Grant. So he had brought Sheridan east with him in March 1864.

Sheridan did not like having his cavalry stuck with the infantry. He complained to Meade, who commanded the Army of the Potomac and was his boss (Grant commanded all of the Union armies and was Meade's boss). Sheridan argued that if Meade let him go, he would "whip" the rebel cavalry, which was commanded by General J. E. B. Stuart. Meade spoke to Grant, and Grant replied, "Did he say so? Then let him go out and do it."

Sheridan told his men, "We are going out to fight Stuart's cavalry.... [W]e will give him a fair, square fight; we are strong, and I know we can beat him.... I shall expect nothing but success." The rebel cavalry had beaten the Union cavalry in all their other battles, but Sheridan's confidence encouraged his men.

Sheridan led his cavalry around Lee's army, then toward Richmond. Stuart soon detected Sheridan's movement, so he led the Confederate cavalry to block him. The two cavalry forces met near Richmond at a place called Yellow Tavern.

The May 11 Battle of Yellow Tavern did not win important ground for the Union. Compared to infantry battles, losses were not heavy. But a Michigan trooper serving with General George

The cavalry battle at Yellow Tavern, Virginia

General James Ewell Brown "Jeb" Stuart

Custer saw a red-bearded rebel officer only twenty-five feet away. He fired his revolver, shooting the officer in the stomach. He did not know that his shot had hit General Stuart.

Stuart died the next day. Back in 1862, Lee had divided the Army of Northern Virginia into three parts. He had given commands to Jackson, Longstreet, and Stuart. Together with these generals, Lee and his army had won worldwide fame. Now the three generals were gone—Jackson dead after Chancellorsville, Longstreet seriously wounded at the Wilderness (although he would recover and return to command), and Stuart dead after Yellow Tavern. The Confederate army could not replace such skilled and experienced commanders.

While Lee's army mourned the loss of Stuart, the Army of the Potomac celebrated the arrival of Phil Sheridan. He had proven himself to be a strong leader. Sheridan's leadership of the Union cavalry showed Grant that he would never have to worry about the Confederate cavalry again. A Union colonel said that the rebel cavalry could hardly compete with the Union cavalry anymore. Because of Sheridan, "our cavalry is full of confidence and does wonders."

One Great Battlefield

While Sheridan advanced toward Richmond, Lee's army beat Grant to Spotsylvania Court House. In the woods around Spotsylvania, the Confederates immediately began building fieldworks (defensive positions using trenches, dirt, and logs) in the woods around Spotsylvania. The land was not as heavily wooded as the Wilderness. A few clearings opened up among the trees.

Lee organized his line of trenches carefully. The Confederates placed artillery all along the line so the guns could fire into the flanks of attacking soldiers. The defending infantry stayed in a deep trench with logs to protect their heads. They could fire and reload their guns without much risk of being shot themselves.

Never before in the history of war had an army in the field prepared a defense like this. From flank to flank, the entire Army of Northern Virginia was behind fieldworks that blocked Grant's way to Spotsylvania. A New Jersey

PHILIP HENRY SHERIDAN

Philip Henry Sheridan was born in New York in 1831 and grew up in Ohio. He went to school at a one-room schoolhouse for only four years. Then he worked as a clerk at a store. Hoping to improve his life, Sheridan talked one of his customers into recommending him for the U.S. Military Academy at West Point. Sheridan graduated from West Point a year late, in 1853, because he got suspended for attacking one of his sergeants with a bayonet. When the man reported him, he attacked him again.

When the Civil War began, Sheridan was working at buying and handing out supplies for the army. In 1862, a friend recommended Sheridan for promotion to colonel of cavalry. He was so good at leading soldiers in battle that he was promoted to general and put in charge of a division only a few weeks later. He was just thirty-one years old at the time. His soldiers called him "Little Phil," because he was very short. He fought in several important battles and bravely led his men in charges against the enemy. Ten years after the war, he married Irene Rucker, the daughter of one of his officers. They had four children.

officer exclaimed, "It is all one great battlefield for miles and miles." No leaders on either side yet understood how difficult it was to attack such a position. They expected that a strong enough charge by a large enough number of men could capture any position.

From May 9 through May 19, the two armies moved and fought around Spotsylvania. When Yankees tried to storm (charge) the trenches on May 10, they lost many men. They tried again with even more men on May 12. The result was some of the fiercest fighting of the war. Their first charge broke through the rebel line. Lee needed time to build a second line of fieldworks. So he ordered his own charge.

Much of the day, the two sides were on opposite sides of Lee's partly built second line of fieldworks. A soldier wrote, "Here on both sides of these breastworks were displayed more individual acts of bravery and heroism than I had yet seen in the war. The graycoats [Confederate soldiers] and bluecoats [Union soldiers] would spring with rifles in hand on top the breastworks, take deadly aim, fire, and then fall across into the trenches below [wounded or killed]. This I saw repeated again and again."

It rained most of the day. The trenches filled with water, bodies, and blood. Unlike most battles, here the men fought at very close range. "It was chiefly a savage hand-to-hand fight across the breastworks," wrote an officer. "Rank after rank was [hit] by shot and shell and bayonet-thrusts, and finally sank, a mass of torn and mutilated corpses. Then fresh troops rushed madly forward to replace the dead, and so the murderous work went on."

The fighting on May 12 continued until midnight. In some places, the dead piled eight or ten bodies deep. The worst fighting took place where the line of breastworks stuck out at an angle. An officer counted 150 bodies in a space less than twelve by fifteen feet. The battle was so awful that history remembered that part of the

Union soldiers storm the breastworks at the Bloody Angle.

A Union officer, standing in water and mud, orders his men forward against the rebel breastworks.

field as "the bloody angle." When the fighting ended, Grant's men had captured about one mile of ground. But the Confederate soldiers' fight had given Lee's army time to build a new line of defenses and then fall back to take cover behind them.

Grant ordered more Union charges over the next days. By the end of May 19, it was clear to Grant that he could not break through Lee's position at Spotsylvania. By the time Grant stopped trying to break through, his army had lost about 17,500 men killed, wounded, and missing during the

Battle of Spotsylvania. Because the Confederates mostly fought from behind their fieldworks, they lost fewer men, probably between 9,000 and 10,000 men. And they still blocked the most direct way to Richmond.

Our Ranks Melt Like Snow under an April Sun

After Spotsylvania, Grant was determined to keep advancing toward Richmond. Again he moved around Lee's flank. Again Lee figured out where he was going and marched to block him. Both sides dug trenches for protection whenever they halted. They became used to living and fighting in these trenches.

An Alabama soldier wrote to his sister, "Though the shells are bursting all around us and the...bullets are cheeping [whistling] just over our heads, we have dug ourselves deep enough into the ground...for me to write a few lines." But Grant's men couldn't stay in the relatively safe trenches. As a Union officer wrote to his family, "Remember, our [purpose] is offense—to advance."

At the beginning of June, the Army of the Potomac faced Lee's army near Richmond at Cold Harbor, Virginia, where the armies had fought in 1862. This time, the Union men knew what to expect when they were ordered to charge the rebels' fieldworks. Large numbers of infantry wrote name tags and pinned them to their backs. This would help the survivors to identify their bodies.

A Louisiana rebel said of Grant, above, "We have met a man this time who either does not know when he is whipped, or who cares not if he loses his whole Army."

Collecting the remains of dead soldiers after the Battle of Cold Harbor

The Battle of Cold Harbor on June 3, 1864, was a disaster for the Union. In less than an hour, 7,500 Union soldiers were casualties. The defenders, protected by breastworks, lost only 1,500 men.

Since the beginning of the campaign in May, the Army of the Potomac had lost about 50,000 men, about 40 percent of its total strength. A New Jersey officer noted, "Our ranks melt away like

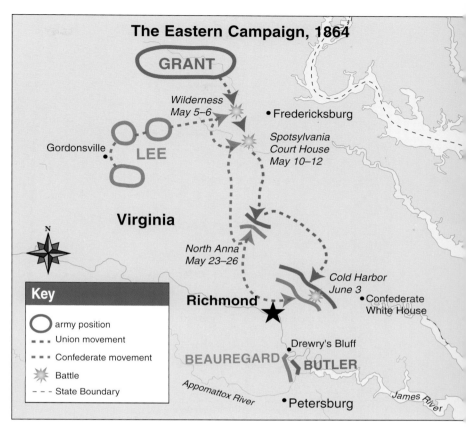

snow under an April sun." Now the Union army's morale, or spirit, collapsed. A newly arrived officer was amazed. He asked, "Don't you believe in Grant at all?" A colonel answered, "Yes, we believe in Grant, but we believe a great deal more in Lee and in that Army of Virginia." Union soldier Oliver Wendell Holmes Jr., who would one day be a U.S. Supreme Court judge, wrote home that, "many a man has gone crazy since this campaign [began] from the terrible pressure on mind and body."

After Cold Harbor, Grant came up with a new plan. Instead of trying to fight through Lee's line, he moved around it. But this time, he did not head toward Richmond. He ordered his army to march quickly to the James River, to cross it, and

to capture Petersburg—a town about twenty miles south of Richmond.

Petersburg was a key railroad center for the Confederate forces in Virginia. If the Union forces captured it, the Confederates would not be able to hold Richmond, because they would lose the railroad linking Richmond with the rest of the South.

On the evening of June 15, a powerful Union force approached the defenders of Petersburg, who were commanded by General Pierre Beauregard. Still unaware of Grant's destination, Lee and his army were elsewhere defending the road to Richmond. This time, Grant had fooled Lee.

A division of black soldiers spearheaded an attack that captured part of Petersburg's defenses. A reporter wrote, "At the word of command, the

Union soldiers in the trenches,
opposite, *at Petersburg,*
Virginia

Dead soldiers at Petersburg,
below

colored men stepped out from the woods, and
stood before the enemy. They gave a volley, and
received one in return. Shells crashed through
them, but . . . with a yell they started up the slope
upon the run. . . . Seventy of their number went
down, but the living hundreds rushed on."

The black troops helped open a one-mile-wide
hole in the Confederate defenses. But their
commander, General William Smith, decided to
wait for reinforcements to arrive instead of
going right through the gap. The next day, about
48,000 Yankees faced only 14,000 defenders.
But the attackers did not know this. They saw
the fieldworks and remembered Cold Harbor
and the other doomed charges. They did not
make much progress against the rebel position.
As one officer later explained, they were
"charged out." Two days later, Lee and his army
caught up with Grant and came to the aid of
Petersburg.

By June 22, Grant realized that his battered
army could not make any more progress against
Lee. All they could do was pin down Lee's army
so it could not march off to fight elsewhere. The
Union men dug trenches and built breastworks.
They settled in for a siege. The two exhausted
armies faced one another on a front running
southward from Richmond to Petersburg. It
seemed that neither army could make the other
budge.

So ended a forty-day-long campaign that cost
both sides a huge number of men. The Union had
lost more than 50,000 men killed, wounded, or
missing. The Confederacy had lost about 30,000
men. The Union army had lost more men, but the
Confederacy did not have enough men left at
home to replace the men its army had lost.

CHAPTER FOUR

The Atlanta Campaign

Union armies everywhere moved forward at the same time the Army of the Potomac entered the Wilderness. Two Union armies invaded Virginia. Political generals commanded both of them.

When the war began, Franz Sigel had helped the Union cause by encouraging German immigrants (newcomers) to fight for the Union. He had been rapidly promoted to general. General Sigel moved south through Virginia's Shenandoah Valley. Confederate general John Breckinridge hastily moved his forces to stop Sigel. The armies met at the Battle of New Market on May 15, 1864. Breckinridge ordered an attack that drove the Yankees from the field. Teenaged Confederate

Four cadets (military students) from the Virginia Military Institute who served at the Battle of New Market. Eighteen-year-old William Butler, far left, survived the battle. Nineteen-year-old Jaqueline Stannard, below left, was killed at the battle. Twenty-year-old Moses Ezekiel, below, carried his wounded friend, seventeen-year-old Thomas G. Jefferson, far right, from the battlefield. Jefferson died from his wounds. Ezekiel later became a famous sculptor. He remembered his friend when he carved a memorial called Virginia Mourning Her Dead.

soldiers from the Virginia Military Institute took part in the day's final charge.

The Confederate victory forced Sigel to retreat, ending his invasion of the Shenandoah Valley. The valley served as a route for armies to cross Virginia to either Washington or Richmond. Breckinridge was able to march through the valley to join Lee and help him defend Richmond. After the Battle of New Market, it was finally clear that Sigel was a hopelessly bad general. Lincoln removed him from command.

Union general Benjamin Butler commanded an army that began the campaign on the Virginia peninsula. He moved his 30,000 men by ship up the James River toward Richmond. Butler ordered his soldiers to land on a small peninsula called Bermuda Hundred, which lay between Richmond and Petersburg. Water surrounds a peninsula on three sides. There was only one way out by land.

Butler did not know that there were only about 5,000 Confederate defenders nearby. He moved cautiously. The Confederate defenders, commanded by General Pierre Beauregard, had time to dig trenches blocking the landward side of Bermuda Hundred. Butler's men were stuck at Bermuda Hundred. Grant wrote that "it was . . . as if Butler was in a bottle [and] the enemy had corked the bottle." A more skilled general would have taken the risk of moving quickly and meeting a large enemy force. However, Butler had been a powerful politician before the war. Lincoln could not afford to replace him.

The armies commanded by Sigel and Butler had failed to help Grant. In the west, another political general, Nathaniel Banks, commanded a Union army. Grant had planned for Banks to march to the important port of Mobile, Alabama. But President Lincoln worried because French troops had arrived in Mexico. He thought they might try to grab American territory. He wanted Banks to invade western Louisiana, move along the Red River, and head for Texas instead.

Banks's Red River campaign failed. Banks moved his forces too slowly, giving the Confederates time to oppose him. He was easily discouraged by obstacles, such as low water that prevented the navy from helping him. Banks had taken 10,000 men from General William T. Sherman's army for this campaign. Sherman never got them back. Also, the 15,000 Confederates defending Mobile saw that they were not

needed because Banks was never going to attack. So the rebels moved to reinforce the Confederate army facing Sherman in Georgia. He would have to face the Confederates on his own.

Sherman Advances

The main campaign in the west began in May 1864. General Sherman commanded Union forces numbering almost 100,000 men. Grant ordered Sherman "to move against [Joseph E.] Johnston's army [and] break it up." Then Sherman was to move into Georgia to inflict "all the damage you can against [the Confederate] war resources."

A veteran company in Sherman's army, Company H, 44th Indiana Infantry Regiment

WILLIAM TECUMSEH SHERMAN

William Tecumseh Sherman was born in Ohio in 1820, one of eleven children. His father, a judge, died when William was nine, leaving his large family without support. Friends of the family, U.S. senator Thomas Ewing and his wife, adopted him and took care of him until he went to the U.S. Military Academy at West Point at the age of sixteen. He graduated in 1840, and he served in the army until 1853. He then resigned because he had become bored with army life.

In 1850, Sherman married Ellen Ewing, the daughter of his adoptive parents. They had eight children. Sherman worked as a banker, a lawyer, and the head of a military school in Louisiana. He liked working at the school, but when the Civil War began, he left the South and rejoined the U.S. Army.

Confederate General Joseph E. Johnston was a skilled and talented officer.

Sherman's army was in excellent shape. During the winter, the soldiers had received good care and lots of food. Officers and men looked forward to the spring campaign with confidence. One general wrote, "Our army is in fine health and spirits and will make one of its best fights this spring." Sherman decided to carry out his orders by capturing Atlanta, Georgia, an important center of transportation and industry for the South.

The Confederate Army of Tennessee stood between Sherman and Atlanta. After losing Chattanooga in 1863, this army retreated to a position in the mountains of northwestern Georgia. The Army of Tennessee was in poor shape. The winter of 1863–1864 was unusually cold for the area. Snow, which rarely fell in Georgia, covered the ground. The soldiers did not have enough food, clothing, shoes, or good shelter. Many men deserted.

A Tennessee soldier wrote, "The morale of the army was gone. The spirit of the soldiers was crushed, their hope gone. The future was dark and gloomy." Then General Joseph E. Johnston was assigned to replace General Braxton Bragg as army commander.

Johnston soon changed things for the better. He made his supply officers do their jobs better, so that his soldiers got more food. He learned that a blockade-runner (a fast ship specially built to move past the Union blockade) had made it into a Southern port with a load of shoes. Johnston sent his supply officers to get thousands of these shoes for his men.

The army's health and spirits improved. In early April, a Confederate officer wrote, "Our men are better clothed than at any [time before], while their food is better than one [could have hoped]." Johnston's soldiers liked their new commander.

A regiment of black soldiers, below. By the time the Civil War ended, about 185,000 blacks had served in the Union army and 29,000 in the Union navy. All black regiments had white officers in charge of them. They did not receive as much pay as white soldiers and sailors. Most of the black regiments did not go into combat and did jobs behind the lines instead. About sixty of the black regiments did fight in battles. Many black soldiers fought bravely, and more than 2,500 lost their lives.

SOLDIERS IN PRISON

In every Civil War battle, some soldiers got captured by the enemy. Early in the war, captured soldiers signed a pledge that they would not fight again for a certain amount of time. Both sides followed strict rules about how long a soldier had to wait. A prisoner had to go home to wait until a prisoner on the other side was traded for him. Then, each man could return to his army.

Sometimes prisoners were taken to prisons in enemy territory. As the war went on, this took place more often. During the war's last two years, the armies no longer exchanged prisoners. Thousands of men lived in prison until the war ended. During the Civil War, about 195,000 Union and 460,000 Confederate soldiers became prisoners of war.

Life in the prisons was hard. A Virginia soldier described life at a federal prison. "We only left the room to march down to the mess-hall. For breakfast we had a cup of poor coffee without milk or sugar, and two small pieces of bad bread. For dinner we had a cup of greasy water [called] soup, a piece of beef two inches square and a half inch thick, and two slices of bread."

In February 1863, 3,884 Confederates were prisoners at Camp Douglas in Chicago, Illinois. Sewage formed standing pools. The prison was so unhealthy that 387 prisoners—one man in ten—died in February. The worst prison in the North was at Elmira, New York. It often flooded. A pool of sewage stood at the center of the prison. It spread disease and death. Only one stove warmed each group of two hundred prisoners. When the prison was the most full, it held over 12,000 men. Ten prisoners died each day. Overall, 2,917 men, one prisoner in four, died at Elmira.

As bad as Elmira was, the South's prisons were worse. The South had trouble feeding its own soldiers. Feeding Yankees was less important, so many prisoners suffered terribly. At least ten of the Confederate prisons were open fields surrounded by high wooden fences. Union prisoners lived without shelter in filthy conditions. A Union prisoner described this type of prison: "As we marched through the gate I could hardly believe it to be possible that this horrible place was to [hold] us even for a few days, and my blood froze with horror as I looked around and saw men who but a short time before enjoyed health and strength, worn down by suffering and disease, until they hardly looked like human beings. Some of them were almost naked, and all were covered with dirt and [insects]."

The soldier's heart sank as he thought, "How can I ever expect to live in this horrible place?"

In fact, many men did not survive in such horrible places. At least 12,912 Union soldiers died at the worst Confederate prison, Andersonville in Georgia. Dozens of prisoners died every day during the fourteen months the prison was open. Andersonville was so bad that, after the war, its commander was arrested. He was put on trial as a war criminal, found guilty, then hanged—the only Civil War officer to come to such an end.

Overall, about 25,976 Confederate and 30,218 Union soldiers died while being held prisoner during the Civil War. Many more died after they were freed because they had been so weakened by hunger and disease.

The Civil War's worst prison, the open stockade at Andersonville in Georgia

Johnston could not solve one major problem. Sherman's army outnumbered Johnston's by about two to one. Even so, for two and a half months, Johnston skillfully used his army to delay the Union advance. He put his army in strong positions and ordered his men to dig trenches and make breastworks. But Sherman did not order his soldiers to charge the breastworks. Instead, he outflanked, or moved around, them.

When Johnston saw that Sherman had outflanked him, he ordered a retreat. Then Johnston set up a new line of defenses to prevent Sherman from advancing. But Sherman kept outflanking him, then advancing toward Atlanta.

Only once did Sherman order a charge against fieldworks. This came on June 27, 1864, at the Battle of Kennesaw Mountain. Sherman mistakenly believed that Kennesaw Mountain was "the key" to unlock this part of Georgia. Sherman also thought his men had grown too cautious, because they stopped moving forward when they saw rebel fieldworks. On June 27, he sent his men up the slope of Kennesaw Mountain. The Union lost about 3,000 men. The Confederates kept control of the ground.

The battle showed Sherman that he should go around Kennesaw Mountain and continue with his flanking moves toward Atlanta. He did this and made slow but steady progress. It took his army seventy-four days to advance about one hundred miles. Still on July 13, Sherman proudly wrote, "Atlanta is in full sight nine miles off."

Johnston defended a very strong position. His army was near its base (the place where the army kept its food and supplies) in Atlanta. Sherman's base at Chattanooga, Tennessee, was far away. A single railroad track connected the Union army with its base. Confederate cavalry might wreck this railroad at any time. Sherman seemed stuck in front of Atlanta like Grant was stuck in front of Petersburg.

CHAPTER FIVE

The Election of 1864

In the North, the 1864 campaign for president was nearing its climax. The Democratic Party chose George McClellan to run against Lincoln. McClellan was a former commander of the Union Army of the Potomac. Lincoln had fired him in 1862 for not attacking the enemy when he had the chance. The Democrats promised to negotiate an end to the war if their candidate became president. If McClellan won the election, the South would gain its independence. Unless the Union forces won important victories before the November election, Northern voters seemed likely to elect McClellan and accept a negotiated peace.

Then came a Confederate attack on the Northern capital, Washington, D.C. Robert E. Lee knew that in the past such threats had alarmed Lincoln. He hoped it would work again and cause Lincoln to order Grant's army to protect the capital. Lee ordered General Jubal Early to move a large force north along the Shenandoah Valley to threaten Washington. Early's men crossed the Potomac River on July 6 to enter Maryland. Early marched toward Washington. His men arrived five miles north of the city on July 11.

Washington had strong defenses, and Grant had sent a large, veteran force to help defend the capital. Early made a careful advance on July 12. During the exchange of gunfire, Lincoln appeared at Fort Stevens to watch. Lincoln, a tall man, was wearing a tall stovepipe hat.

Union general George McClellan was the Democratic candidate in the 1864 election.

The Democratic and Republican Parties in 1864

The Republican Party was still new in 1864. Antislavery politicians had begun calling themselves Republicans in 1854. Abraham Lincoln's election as president in 1860 marked the first time in U.S. history that a Republican candidate won the presidency.

But members of the same American political party did not always agree on how the president should govern the nation. Different groups formed within each party. As the Civil War continued and the Union army lost battles, Lincoln faced harsh criticism not only from the Democrats, but from his own party as well. The Republicans supported continuing the Civil War until the North won.

Lincoln was a moderate Republican. Radical Republicans thought he was not fighting the war aggressively enough. They wanted to nominate a Union army general, such as Grant or Sherman, to be the Republican candidate for president in 1864. When the Union army won battles in 1864, the Republican Party kept Lincoln as its candidate.

Before the Civil War, many Southerners had belonged to the Democratic Party. During the Civil War, the Democratic Party split between "Peace Democrats," who wanted to end the war immediately, and "War Democrats." If they wanted to win the 1864 presidential election, the two factions (groups) had to work out an agreement. The Democrats nominated the former Union general, George McClellan, a War Democrat, for president. They let the Peace Democrats write the party platform (a statement of what the party's candidates would do if elected).

The Democratic platform called for an immediate cease-fire and negotiations to end to the war. It described the war as a failure. Candidate McClellan did not agree with the platform. He wrote, "I could not look in the faces of gallant comrades of the army and navy . . . and tell them that their labor and the sacrifice of our slain and wounded brethren had been in vain." This letter angered the Peace Democrats, and some wanted to choose another candidate. The party decided that McClellan was the best candidate.

Confederate bullets whizzed past Lincoln. A Union captain did not recognize the president. But he saw the danger. He shouted, "Get down, you damn fool, before you get shot!" Lincoln sat down.

Early decided that Washington was too well defended for his army to attack successfully. So he ordered a return to Virginia. His raid on Washington ended. But he attacked several places in Virginia, Maryland, and Pennsylvania. Grant put Sheridan in charge of a 48,000-man army, then sent him to the Shenandoah Valley to stop Early.

The Crater
Meanwhile, the siege of Petersburg continued. After the hard fighting, both Grant's and Lee's armies were exhausted.

The Union soldiers could not charge the defenses of Petersburg. So the commander of a regiment made up mostly of former Pennsylvania coal miners had the idea of digging a long tunnel under the Confederate trenches.

Fort Stevens, where President Lincoln came under fire, was one of several Union forts around Washington, D.C., the nation's capital. This photograph shows the guns of Fort Totten, another fort defending Washington.

Grant approved the idea. The soldiers spent about one month digging a 511-foot-long tunnel and filling it with 8,000 pounds of gunpowder. On July 30, they blew it up.

The explosion destroyed part of the rebel line and left a huge pit, or crater. Nearly 300 defenders were killed or wounded. Many others were dazed by the blast. Union infantry were supposed to charge through the 500-yard-wide gap in the Confederate line.

But the two Union generals in charge stayed in the rear. The soldiers did not know what to do without leaders. Three divisions of soldiers, including one of black soldiers, moved forward and filled the crater. Then they found that they could not crawl up the thirty-foot-high bank at the far side.

The Confederates brought weapons from their lines to shell the helpless Yankees. Rebel infantry poured gunfire into the crater. The Confederates fought with particular savagery because they

The rebel counterattack into the crater

hated black soldiers. They took no black prisoners, but killed them instead.

By day's end, the Union had lost another 4,400 men. Grant called the Battle of the Crater "the saddest affair I have witnessed in the war." A New York patriot wrote on August 19, "I see no bright spot anywhere. . . . I fear the blood and treasure spent on this summer's campaign have done little for the country."

Grant's army had suffered terrible losses. On July 18, 1864, Lincoln followed up the previous year's draft with a second call for 500,000 men. The draft was so unpopular that Democratic politicians thought it would help them win the November election.

The Battle of Mobile Bay

On August 5, 1864, Admiral David Farragut led his Union navy fleet against Mobile, Alabama, a major Southern port still controlled by the Confederates. Farragut commanded fourteen

Admiral David Farragut, standing in the rigging, was a fearless naval leader. He had joined the navy when he was nine years old.

wooden ships and four ironclads (ships protected by iron armor). They tried to run by the powerful fort that protected Mobile Bay. The fort and the fleet exchanged terrific gunfire. In the water, the Confederates also had placed explosive charges (called mines in modern times, but known as torpedoes during the Civil War). The leading ironclad hit a torpedo and sank. Ninety-three sailors went down with their ship.

The ships halted, fearing to sail through the mines. Farragut refused to retreat. He shouted the most famous naval order of the war: "Damn the torpedoes! Full speed ahead."

Farragut's own ship took the lead. The rest of the fleet followed him safely among the mines into Mobile Bay. Inside the bay, a small rebel fleet included the CSS *Tennessee,* a giant ironclad. Admiral Frank Buchanan (the same officer who, in 1862, had commanded the CSS *Virginia,* the South's first ironclad) commanded the *Tennessee.* Buchanan led a brave but hopeless fight. Farragut's fleet pounded the *Tennessee* until the vessel surrendered.

Farragut's victory at Mobile Bay closed off the only Confederate port on the Gulf of Mexico outside Texas. Slowly the Union navy closed its grip on the Confederate seacoast.

The victory in far-off Alabama did not seem very important to many Northerners, compared to the discouraging situations in Georgia and Virginia. It was still not clear who would win the presidential election, Lincoln or McClellan. Lincoln believed that he would lose. On August 23 he wrote, "This morning . . . it seems [very] likely that this Administration will not be re-elected." He told an officer, "I am going to be beaten. . . . and unless some great change takes place."

An Indiana soldier described his unit's part in the Battle of Atlanta, below, *on July 22: "The 97th [Regiment] fought in three different places and on each side of our works, for the attack was on front and rear. . . . We killed, in front of our regiment, one colonel and major and one captain within fifteen feet of our lines. . . . The rebel colonel was shot full of holes twenty feet from where I was."*

Jefferson Davis made a terrible decision when he chose John Hood, above, *to replace Joe Johnston.*

A Great Change

Jefferson Davis had mistrusted General Joe Johnston for a long time. Back in 1862, Johnston had retreated all the way up the Virginia peninsula from Yorktown to Richmond. He might have abandoned Richmond if he had not received a wound. Lee took his place and held firm.

Now it seemed that Johnston was retreating again in Georgia. As Sherman kept marching around his army, Johnston kept falling back and building new fieldworks. He wanted to save his soldiers for a fight at a time of his own choosing. But Davis was afraid that Johnston would not fight to save Atlanta.

On July 17, Davis replaced Johnston with General John Hood. Hood was one of the most aggressive leaders in the entire war. He bravely led his men and was often at the front of the fighting. This behavior had already given Hood two serious wounds, which caused the loss of a leg and a crippled arm.

Hood knew why President Davis chose him to lead the army. Davis wanted Hood to fight. So Hood ordered a series of furious attacks. They began on July 20, when Hood ordered his army to attack Sherman at Peachtree Creek. The Union forces caused heavy losses on the Confederate side and drove them off. But Hood did not give up. Two days later, he attacked again. At the July 22 Battle of Atlanta, Union forces again defeated the Confederates, causing even heavier losses.

Finally on July 28, Hood attacked for a third time. The Battle of Ezra Church was a third defeat. In eight days, Hood had lost more men than Johnston had lost during seventy-four days. Hood's fierce attacks shattered the Confederate Army of Tennessee. By September 1, Hood withdrew his army and abandoned Atlanta. As the rebels left, they set fire to the military supplies stored in the city.

The Atlanta campaign cost the Union forces 21,656 men. The Confederates lost 27,565 killed, wounded, and captured.

Sherman then sent one of the most famous messages of the entire war. He telegraphed President Lincoln, "Atlanta is ours and fairly won." This important victory helped Lincoln in his election contest with McClellan.

A headline in a Republican newspaper asked, "Is the War a Failure?" It then said that the capture of Atlanta was "Old Abe's Reply." A Union patriot wrote in his diary, "Glorious news this morning—Atlanta taken at last!!!.... The greatest event of the war."

The ruins of Atlanta, right. A ten-year-old Atlanta girl wrote in her diary on November 12, "We were frightened almost to death last night. Some mean soldiers set several houses on fire in different parts of the town." Two days later, she wrote, "They came burning Atlanta today."

Hood's ammunition train was destroyed in Atlanta. A Virginia private wrote in his diary, "Heard of the fall of Atlanta. The future looks dark and hopeless for the South."

Sheridan in the Valley

In August, Grant had put General Phil Sheridan in charge of the Union forces in the Shenandoah Valley. His orders to Sheridan were to destroy Early's Confederate army.

Sheridan began carefully. For six weeks, no battles took place. Then a Union spy, Rebecca Wright, told Sheridan that an important part of Early's army had left the valley. Sheridan decided to attack.

On September 19, about 37,000 Yankees attacked Early's 15,000 men at Winchester, Virginia. The battle was hard fought. The outnumbered rebels were finally beaten badly with the loss of about one-quarter of Early's army.

Sheridan chased Early hard. Early's men dug trenches at a place called Fisher's Hill. On September 22, Sheridan ordered some of his men to feint, or fake, an attack against the trenches. Then a powerful force burst out of the woods and attacked Early's flank. The Battle of Fisher's Hill was another Union victory.

51

Union general Philip Sheridan, right. *A popular poem,* Sheridan's Ride, *by Thomas Buchanan Read describes the Battle of Cedar Creek. It begins:*

Up from the South, at break of day,
Bringing to Winchester fresh dismay...
The terrible grumble, and rumble, and roar,
Telling the battle was on once more,
And Sheridan twenty miles away.

The poem ends:

The first that the general saw were the groups
Of stragglers, and then the retreating troops...
He dashed down the line, 'mid a storm of huzzas,
And the wave of retreat checked its course there, because,
The sight of the master compelled it to pause.
With foam and with dust the black charger was gray;
By the flash of his eye, and his red nostril's play,
He seemed to the whole great army to say:
"I have brought you Sheridan all the way
From Winchester down to save the day."

Hurrah! hurrah for Sheridan!
Hurrah! hurrah for horse and man!

The war turned ugly in the Shenandoah Valley, known as "The Breadbasket of the Confederacy." The valley's farms had longed served to feed Lee's army. Grant told Sheridan, "If the war is to last another year, we want the Shenandoah Valley to remain a barren waste." Grant ordered Sheridan to destroy things "so that crows flying over it . . . will have to carry their [food] with them."

As autumn began, the Yankees set to burning and destroying. In a short period of time, they destroyed over 2,000 barns filled with wheat and farm tools, 70 mills filled with flour, and they killed more than 4,000 cattle and 3,000 sheep. Sheridan said, "The people must be left with nothing but their eyes to weep with over the war." The people who lived in the valley forever remembered this time as "the Great Burning."

On October 19, General Early made a surprise attack against Sheridan. At first the attack went well. The Confederates captured the Union camps and drove the Yankees back across the field in confusion.

Sheridan himself was in Winchester, about eighteen miles north of the battle. When he heard the sounds of battle, he mounted his famous black horse and galloped south. Sheridan was one of those rare leaders who could rally his men by the force of his personality. When he saw the men retreating, he called, "Turn back! Face the other way! . . . if I had been there this morning this wouldn't have happened! You'll have your own camps back before night."

Everywhere Sheridan appeared, his men sprang up and cheered. To one group of soldiers, Sheridan shouted, "Jubal Early drive me out of the valley? I'll lick him like blazes before night! I'll give him the worst licking he ever had!" And that is what Sheridan did. His arrival inspired his men, and he led them to attack the rebels. The October 19 Battle of Cedar Creek destroyed Early's army so it could never fight again. One in six of Early's men became casualties. The surviving men scattered, and Sheridan captured most of Early's guns, ammunition, wagons, and food.

News of Sherman's capture of Atlanta, Farragut's victory at Mobile Bay, and Sheridan's three victories in the Shenandoah Valley spread throughout the North. Voters saw that the war might end soon in victory for the North. They reelected Lincoln. Lincoln's reelection ended the South's last hope for victory.

After the fall of Atlanta, Confederate president Jefferson Davis had said, "We are fighting for existence; and by fighting alone can independence be gained." The reelection of Lincoln did nothing to change his mind.

CHAPTER SIX

Appomattox and Beyond

>─◆>─○─<◆─<

Union soldiers drink, wash, and cool their blistered feet after a hard march.

The fighting continued. In Georgia, the Confederate general John Hood tried another bold strategy. Hood hoped that he could give the Confederacy a major victory. He marched around Sherman's army, then headed for Sherman's rear. Sherman sent General George Thomas with a force to defend his rear.

Hood's invasion of Tennessee led to the Battle of Franklin on November 30, 1864. Before the battle, Hood had written to the Confederate government, blaming his men for losing Atlanta. Hood's men knew what he thought of them. To prove their courage, his army attacked with desperate bravery. The rebels charged across two miles of open ground against a Union force defending breastworks. The result was slaughter. Hood's army lost 6,252 men, while the defenders lost only 2,326.

Hood's wounded army continued to Nashville, Tennessee. It was too weak to capture this Union base. General Thomas commanded the Union soldiers there. The Yankees outnumbered the rebels more than two to one. Thomas prepared carefully and made an excellent plan to attack Hood. The Battle of Nashville (December 15–16, 1864) was a great Union victory. Hood retreated south to Mississippi with the remains of his army. Then he sorrowfully resigned his command.

Southerners realized that the end was near. A Confederate official wrote, "things are getting worse very rapidly." About a week after the battle, Lincoln spoke to the U.S. Congress: "We are gaining strength, and may, if need be, maintain the contest indefinitely."

Meanwhile, Sherman decided to march through enemy territory from Atlanta to Savannah, Georgia, a port on the Atlantic Ocean. His soldiers would carry only ammunition and medicine. They would take food from the civilians who lived along the way. Sherman's plan was to destroy everything in Georgia that might help the Confederate soldiers keep fighting.

Sherman left Atlanta on November 15, 1864. There were no Confederate forces that could stop Sherman's March to the Sea. During the march, the Yankees burned buildings and took food and valuables from people's homes. Some Union officers tried to control their men and to keep them from harming women and children. Others lost all control. Many Union soldiers, far from home, seemed to enjoy taking revenge on civilians for all they had suffered during the Civil War.

One Southerner wrote, "Stables were torn down, smoke-houses invaded and emptied of all their bacon and hams: chicken[s] were [eaten], vehicles of all kinds were taken or destroyed, barrels of sugar or molasses were emptied—the sugar carried off, while the molasses ran in

This illustration shows Sherman's men in Georgia. The men in the background are burning and looting the barn and equipment. An Illinois private described how he and his comrades stole from the countryside. He wrote, "The people along the road would tie their horses and mules in swamps, drive their cattle, sheep and hogs onto islands in the swamp. Buried all of their clothes, corn, salt pork, jewelry, money. . . . But they were found by the . . . Yankees, after all."

streams in the yard." After Sherman's men had marched through Georgia, a girl described the result: "There was hardly a fence left standing. . . . The fields were trampled down, and the road was lined with [dead bodies] of horses, hogs, and cattle. . . . The [houses] that were standing all showed signs of [robbery], and on every plantation we saw the charred remains of the [cotton] gin houses."

By December 10, Sherman reached Savannah. When his army captured the city, he sent a message to President Lincoln. "I beg to present you, as a Christmas gift, the city of Savannah, with 150 heavy guns and . . . about 25,000 bales of cotton." The message reached Lincoln on Christmas Eve.

Sherman was now close to South Carolina. His army was in position to march northward through South Carolina and North Carolina and then into Lee's rear in Virginia. He and Grant agreed that Grant would continue to hammer Lee at Petersburg while Sherman marched against Lee's rear. Then together the two large Union armies would crush Lee.

The winter of 1864–1865 was very hard on Southern soldiers. A Virginia private wrote, "The future looks gloomy, almost hopeless. I wonder if I shall live to see 1866. I do not believe I shall."

Jefferson Davis still refused to give up. He said, "The war came, and now it must go on till the last man of this generation falls in his tracks, and his children seize his musket and fight our battle."

Davis promoted Robert E. Lee to general in chief of the Armies of the Confederate States in January 1865. Lee had the authority to command all of the Confederacy's remaining soldiers. But it was too late. Even if all the South's armies joined together, Lee had fewer than 200,000 men. Grant

Columbia, South Carolina, after it was burned by Sherman's men

had more than one million. Still, Lee tried to follow his president's orders and keep fighting.

Beginning on February 1, 1865, as soon as the worst of the winter weather had cleared, Sherman marched his army north through the Carolinas. Only a few troops sent east from Hood's shattered army—now commanded by General Joseph Johnston—stood between Sherman and his goal. They fought Sherman several times but were always outnumbered and driven back.

Sherman wrote, "Somehow, our men had got the idea that South Carolina was the cause of all our troubles. . . . [H]er people had been in a great hurry to [push] the country into civil war; and therefore on them should fall the [suffering] of war in its worst form . . . so that I saw and felt that we would not be able longer to restrain our men as we had done in Georgia." Sherman's men indeed continued to burn, loot, and destroy Southern property as they marched through the Carolinas.

The last campaign in Virginia began on March 27, 1865. Grant's and Lee's armies still manned a line of fortifications from Richmond to Petersburg. Grant ordered Sheridan to take a large force and move around Lee's right flank. Sheridan defeated General George Pickett at the Battle of Five Forks on April 1, 1865. The Union forces could then surround Petersburg. Lee knew he could no longer hold Petersburg and Richmond. The next morning, he warned President Davis that the Confederates would have to evacuate the cities.

When Grant heard about Sheridan's success at Five Forks, he ordered an assault all along the line early on April 2. Lee's defenders were spread far too thinly. The Yankees overran the Confederate line, forcing them to retreat. The last Confederate troops left Petersburg late at night on April 2.

For almost ten months, a Pennsylvania soldier had served in the trenches. For ten months, he had seen the church steeples of Petersburg. Now he and his unit marched into the town. They crossed the Confederate fortifications and trenches. He shared his thoughts with his mother: "No one could help thinking . . . if they [the rebels] could not hold such fortifications as they had there, surely they cannot make a stand anywhere. The fighting is almost over."

Confederate troops also abandoned Richmond the night of April 2. They set fire to weapons and supplies to keep them out of Union hands. The fire spread to destroy much of the city. President Davis and members of the Confederate government fled Richmond and headed south. On April 4, President Lincoln visited the fallen capital of the Confederacy.

Lee and his army marched west. They hoped to find food, then to turn south to join forces with General Johnston's army in North Carolina. Lee

Union soldiers storm a Confederate position defending Petersburg. After Five Forks, the Confederates were too weak to hold the lines at Petersburg.

The ruins of Richmond, the capital of the Confederacy

hoped that, together with Johnston, he could defeat Sherman's army, then return to defeat Grant.

Grant chased hard to prevent Lee's army from reaching Johnston's army. Grant caught up with Lee, and the armies fought two small battles on April 6 and 7. The rebels could not escape. More than 100,000 Union soldiers surrounded about 26,000 Confederates near Appomattox Court House on April 9. Lee surrendered his army.

Grant treated the surrendered rebels generously. He did not take them prisoner or try to punish them. He only made them promise to stop fighting and return home. He let them keep their swords, pistols, and most important, their horses. With the war almost over, Grant knew they would need horses to plow their fields to grow food after the war. He also gave Lee's hungry soldiers food. Grant was more interested in restoring peace than in having revenge. Lee urged his men to honor the surrender, give up the fight, and return home.

The honorable behavior of Lee and Grant set the pattern for all Confederate surrenders. One

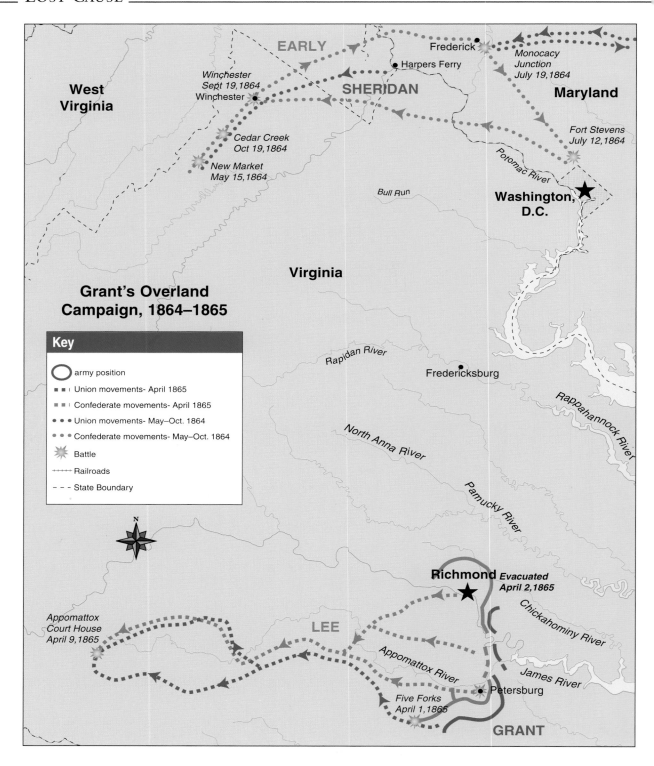

Grant's Overland Campaign, 1864–1865

Key

○ army position
■ ■ ■ Union movements- April 1865
■ ■ ■ Confederate movements- April 1865
● ● ● Union movements- May–Oct. 1864
● ● ● Confederate movements- May–Oct. 1864
✹ Battle
┼┼┼┼ Railroads
– – – State Boundary

by one, the remaining rebel forces surrendered. When Johnston, in North Carolina, heard of Lee's surrender to Grant, he surrendered his army to Sherman on April 26. As the news traveled south and west, Confederate forces surrendered in Alabama on May 4, Arkansas on May 11, and Florida on May 17. Two last surrenders took place in the far west in late May and in June.

A National Tragedy

Less than a week after Lee's surrender, on the night of April 14, 1865, came a horrible event that no one expected. Abraham Lincoln was

Victorious Union soldiers proudly return to New York carrying their battle flag.

seeing a play at Ford's Theatre in Washington, D.C. John Wilkes Booth, a man who thought of himself as a Confederate agent, shot and killed Lincoln. Shouting, "The South is avenged," Booth escaped from the theater. Union forces cornered and killed Booth on April 26.

Lincoln's death was a national tragedy. Lincoln was the one American who might have healed the wounds between the North and the South. He had developed a plan to let each former Confederate state back into the Union as soon as it ended slavery and pledged loyalty to the United States. This plan was called "Reconstruction," or rebuilding the Union. Many Northern politicians had disagreed with Lincoln. They wanted to punish the South and make it harder for the Southern states to rejoin the Union. But Lincoln was a strong leader who might have gotten them to change their minds.

After Lincoln's death, U.S. congressmen argued with the new president, Andrew Johnson, over how to treat the South and the former slaves. While politicians argued, violent fights broke out over how to treat freed blacks. Many Southern whites did not want the freed blacks to have equal rights with whites. So they formed groups like the Ku Klux Klan. Klan members went out at night to attack, and sometimes kill, blacks and the Northern whites who helped them.

A former slave reported, "The Ku Klux got so bad, us had to move back with Mr. Nelson for protection. The men that took us in was Union men. They lived here in the south but they took [our side]. . . . The Ku Klux threatened to whup Mr. Nelson because he took up for the [blacks]. Heap of nights we would hear of the Ku Klux coming and leave home. Sometimes we [were] scared not to go and scared to go."

A Union soldier returns home after the war.

The Civil War had touched nearly every family in the nation. One out of every ten able-bodied Northern males died or was wounded. For the South, one in three men died or was wounded.

The Civil War created a new duty for all Americans. On March 3, 1863, the U.S. Congress had passed the Enrollment Act, the nation's first draft law. This law made all able-bodied males between twenty and forty-five years of age take the chance of serving in the military. The Enrollment Act changed American history. Before, only the states had the power to order their citizens to fight a war. The Enrollment Act gave the U.S. government the power to say that every American citizen has the duty to defend the nation.

The Civil War also ended slavery in the United States. Black Americans were free. Their long struggle for equal rights began. And Lincoln had accomplished his main goal, to save the Union. No state has since tried to withdraw from the United States. The United States remains one nation. But its people have not forgotten the Civil War or the questions that divided them.

What Happened to Them after the War?

>─┤─◆>─○─<◆>─┤─<

Jefferson Davis, president of the Confederate States of America, along with members of his government, left Richmond after Lee surrendered the city. He hoped to make it across the Mississippi River to Texas and continue the war. On May 10, 1865, Davis was captured in Georgia and put in prison. He was considered a criminal and charged with treason. His health was damaged by harsh treatment and by living in a cold, damp cell. After two years, he was released and went to Canada, where he tried to recover his health. The U.S. government never actually tried him for treason. The charges were dropped in 1868.

Davis traveled to Europe to look for a job. He also was offered the presidency of several Southern colleges, but the jobs didn't pay enough for him to support his wife and children. He worked for a few years for an insurance company in Tennessee.

Many people in the South continued to love and admire Davis. One of his admirers gave him a home in Mississippi. He moved there and wrote a book called *The Rise and Fall of the Confederate Government.* He lived to be eighty-one years old.

Ulysses S. Grant stayed on as head of the U.S. Army after the Civil War. He traveled throughout the South. When he returned to Washington, he urged the U.S. government to treat the South kindly. He later became the U.S. secretary of war. When some politicians urged that Lee and his officers be arrested for treason, Grant threatened to resign. In 1868, a grateful nation elected Grant president of the United States. Grant coined the Republican Party campaign slogan, "Let us have peace." He won a second term four years later.

After his presidency, Grant spent two years traveling around the world. In 1884, he lost his money in a business that failed. He then wrote a book about his life to try to make back some of the money. He finished the book a few days before he died in 1885 at the age of sixty-three. *Personal Memoirs* by U. S. Grant was a good book, and many people bought it. The book made a lot of money for his widow and children. After Grant died, Mrs. Grant lived in New York. She became a close friend of Varina Davis, wife of Jefferson Davis.

Robert E. Lee took the job of president of Washington College in Virginia. He needed the job to support his wife and seven children. He ran the college very well and served as a good example to the students. A loyal American before and after the Civil War, Lee encouraged his students to be good citizens of both Virginia and the United States of America. He worked at Washington College until he died in 1870 at the age of sixty-three. Both Lee and his favorite horse, Traveller, are buried there. In 1871, the college was renamed Washington & Lee in his honor.

William T. Sherman replaced Ulysses S. Grant as commanding general of the U.S. Army when Grant became president in 1869. Sherman stayed in that job until

1883. He retired from the army in 1884. He died in 1891 at the age of seventy-one. He wrote a book about his life called *Memoirs of General W. T. Sherman*.

Blacks were freed from slavery by the end of the Civil War. Slavery was officially ended by the Thirteenth Amendment to the U.S. Constitution on December 6, 1865. Life for many freed slaves was a struggle for survival.

Former slaves had to learn to support themselves by farming or working at jobs. "We ain't never been what I calls free.... [We] still have to work just as hard, and sometimes have less than we used to have when we stay on Marse John's plantation." A few who had been treated well by their owners stayed on their plantations as low-paid farm laborers.

Others left to live and work elsewhere. One said, "After the surrender I didn't have to do any more cotton picking and I went blacksmithing for Joe Sturgis. ... Now my son done took on the work." Hard work improved life for many freedmen and their families. A carpenter reported, "There's two of my sons what's doctors; one is a carpenter.... My gals is doing fine, too. Three of them is been school teachers."

Some freed slaves whose family members had been sold traveled in search of them. Only a few ever found their lost parents, children, brothers, and sisters.

The South had a hard time recovering from the Civil War. Southerners mourned the many men who had died. They struggled to rebuild the houses and barns that had been destroyed and to replant their ruined fields. Both blacks and whites in the South lived in poverty for many years after the Civil War.

Many white Southerners blamed black people for their troubles. They falsely accused black people of crimes. White Southerners passed laws controlling where black Southerners could go and what they could do and tried to stop them from voting. Southern whites formed secret societies like the Ku Klux Klan to threaten and harm black people. A former slave described how freed slaves lived in fear. "The Ku Klux got so bad that they would even get us in the daytime. They took some of the [blacks] and throwed them in the river to drown. They kept this up till some folks from the North come down and put a stop to it."

Many white Southerners resented the white Northerners who came to the South to help freed slaves and to organize new state governments. Southerners called these Northerners "carpetbaggers," after the type of luggage they carried. While some carpetbaggers did work to help Southern blacks, many others were only interested in helping themselves.

During Reconstruction, many new schools opened in the South, bringing public education to some areas for the first time. White children and black children had separate schools for nearly one hundred years. Not until 1870 did all the former Confederate states set up governments approved by the U.S. Congress and rejoin the nation.

Time Line

><->-O-<->-<

May 5–6, 1864: The Battle of the Wilderness, in Virginia.

May 9–19, 1864: The Spotsylvania campaign, in Virginia. Both sides lose thousands of soldiers during several battles, but the Union army is unable to defeat the Confederates.

May 15, 1864: Battle of New Market, Virginia. Teenaged cadets from the Virginia Military Institute help the Confederates to win.

June 3, 1864: Second Battle of Cold Harbor, near Richmond, Virginia. Grant's army loses badly because his soldiers have to charge against soldiers in trenches.

June 27, 1864: Sherman's Union army loses the Battle of Kennesaw Mountain, Georgia.

July 30, 1864: Union soldiers set off a large explosion outside Petersburg, Virginia, killing many Confederate soldiers and forming a huge crater. But the Union army is unable to make any progress in their Siege of Petersburg, which lasts from June 1864 to almost the end of the Civil War.

August 5, 1864: Admiral Farragut wins a Union naval victory at Mobile Bay, Alabama.

September 1, 1864: After several battles, Sherman's Union army captures Atlanta, Georgia.

September 19, 1864: The Union wins at the Battle of Winchester, Virginia.

October 19, 1864: Sheridan's Union cavalry defeats the Confederates at the Battle of Cedar Creek, Virginia.

November 8, 1864: Abraham Lincoln wins reelection as president of the United States.
November 15–December 10, 1864: Sherman's "March to the Sea." The Union army marches from Atlanta to Savannah, Georgia, destroying property along the way.

November 30, 1864: Confederate general Hood and his army are defeated at the Battle of Franklin, Tennessee.

December 15–16, 1864: Hood loses again at the Battle of Nashville, Tennessee.

April 1, 1865: Sheridan's Union cavalry and infantry defeat Pickett at the Battle of Five Forks, Virginia.

April 2–3, 1865: The Confederate army surrenders Richmond, Virginia, to the Union army.

April 9, 1865: Robert E. Lee surrenders his Confederate army to U.S. Grant at Appomattox Court House, Virginia.

April 14, 1865: John Wilkes Booth kills President Lincoln at Ford's Theatre in Washington, D.C. Vice President Andrew Johnson becomes president.

April 26, 1865: Confederate general Joseph Johnston surrenders his army to Sherman.

June 2, 1865: The last Confederate soldiers surrender to the Union in Texas.

Notes

For quoted material in text:

p. 6, J. Roderick Heller, III and Carolynn Ayres Heller, ed., *The Confederacy Is on Her Way Up the Spout: Letters to South Carolina 1861–1864* (Athens: The University of Georgia Press, 1992), 115.

p. 6, William H. Runge, ed., *Four Years in the Confederate Artillery: The Diary of Private Henry Robinson Berkeley* (Richmond: Virginia Historical Society, 1991), 65.

p. 11, Gary W. Gallagher, ed., *The Wilderness Campaign* (Chapel Hill: University of North Carolina Press, 1997), 38.

p. 13, Francis A. Lord, *They Fought for the Union* (New York: Bonanza Books, 1960), 225.

p. 13, Richard Wheeler, *On Fields of Fury: From the Wilderness to the Crater, An Eyewitness History* (New York: Harper Collins Publishers, 1991), 54.

p. 13, Ulysses S. Grant, *Personal Memoirs* (1885; reprint New York: Da Capo Press, 1982), 369.

p. 16, Tyler Dennett, ed., *Lincoln and the Civil War in the Diaries and Letters of John Hay* (New York: Dodd, Mead, & Co., 1939), 179.

p. 18, George R. Agassiz, ed., *Meade's Headquarters 1863–1865: Letters of Colonel Theodore Lyman from the Wilderness to Appomattox* (Boston: Massachusetts Historical Society, 1922), 101.

p. 18, Ibid., 89.

p. 19, Horace Porter, *Campaigning with Grant* (New York: The Century Co., 1897), 70.

p. 19, Gallagher, ed., *The Wilderness Campaign*, 176.

p. 20, Ibid., 177.

p. 20, Richard Wheeler, *Voices of the Civil War* (New York: Thomas Y. Crowell Co., 1976), 387.

p. 21, Ibid., 390.

p. 22, John B. Gordon, *Reminiscences of the Civil War* (New York: Charles Scribner's Sons, 1903), 268–269.

p. 22, Philip H. Sheridan, *Personal Memoirs of P. H. Sheridan*, vol. 1 (New York: Charles L. Webster & Co., 1888), 369.

p. 23, Sheridan, *Personal Memoirs of P. H. Sheridan*, vol. 1, 370.

p. 24, Agassiz, ed., *Meade's Headquarters 1863-1865*, 131.

p. 26, James I. Robertson, ed., *The Civil War Letters of General Robert McAllister* (New Brunswick, NJ: Rutgers University Press, 1965), 422.

p. 26, Ibid., 419.

p. 26, Porter, *Campaigning with Grant*, 110.

p. 29, Annette Tapert, ed., *The Brothers' War: Civil War Letters to Their Loved Ones from the Blue and Gray* (New York: Times Books, 1988), 197.

p. 29, Agassiz, ed., *Meade's Headquarters 1863-1865*, 100.

pp. 30–31, Robertson, ed., *The Civil War Letters of General Robert McAllister*, 427.

p. 31, James R. Arnold, *The Armies of U. S. Grant* (London: Arms and Armour Press, 1995), 221.

p. 31, Ibid.

pp. 32–33, Charles Carleton Coffin, *The Boys of '61: or, Four Years of Fighting; Personal Observation With the Army and Navy, From the First Battle of Bull Run to the Fall of Richmond* (Boston: Dana Estes and Co., 1896), 316.

p. 33, Robertson, ed., *The Civil War Letters of General Robert McAllister*, 445.

p. 36, Grant, *Personal Memoirs*, 377.

p. 37, Vincent J. Esposito, ed., *The West Point Atlas of the American Wars*, vol. 1 (New York: Frederick A. Praeger Publishers, 1964), 145.

p. 38, James Lee McDonough and James Pickett Jones, *War So Terrible: Sherman and Atlanta* (New York: W. W. Norton and Co., 1987), 44.

p. 39, Samuel R. Watkins, *"Co. Aytch; A Sideshow of the Big Show"*, (New York: Collier Books, 1962), 126.

p. 39, McDonough and Jones, *War So Terrible* (New York: W. W. Norton & Co., 1987), 56.

p. 42, William Tecumseh Sherman, *Memoirs of General W. T. Sherman* (New York: The Library of America, 1990), 530.

p. 42, Joseph H. Ewing, *Sherman at War* (Dayton, OH: Morningside House, 1992), 130.

p. 45, James M. McPherson, *Battle Cry of Freedom* (New York: Oxford University Press, 1988), 757.

p. 47, U. S. Grant to H. Halleck, 1 August 1864, in *War of the Rebellion: Official Records of the Union and Confederate Armies*, vol. 40, part I (Washington, D.C.: Government Printing Office, 1892), 17.

p. 47, Allan Nevins and Milton Halsey Thomas, eds., *The Diary of George Templeton Strong* (New York: Macmillan Co., 1952), 474.

p. 48, *Battles and Leaders of the Civil War*, vol. 4 (New York: Thomas Yoseloff, 1956), 391.

p. 48, Roy C. Basler, ed., *The Collected Works of Abraham Lincoln*, vol. 7 (New Brunswick, NJ: Rutgers University Press, 1953), 514.

p. 48, McPherson, *Battle Cry of Freedom*, 771.

p. 50, W. T. Sherman to H. Halleck, 3 September 1864, in *War of the Rebellion: Official Records of the Union and Confederate Armies*, vol. 38, part V (Washington, D.C.: Government Printing Office, 1891), 777.

p. 50, Nevins and Thomas, eds., *The Diary of George Templeton Strong*, 480-481.

p. 52, U. S. Grant to P. Sheridan, 26 August 1864, in *War of the Rebellion: Official Records of the Union and Confederate Armies*, vol. 43, part II (Washington, D.C.: Government Printing Office, 1893), 202.

p. 52, U.S. Grant to H. Halleck, 14 July 14 1864, in *War of the Rebellion: Official Records of the Union and Confederate Armies*, vol. 40, part III (Washington, D.C.: Government Printing Office, 1892), 223.

p. 52, McPherson, *Battle Cry of Freedom*, 778.

p. 53, Bruce Catton, *A Stillness at Appomattox* (Garden City, NY: Doubleday and Co., 1953), 312.

p. 53, Ibid., 315.

p. 53, McPherson, *Battle Cry of Freedom*, 806.

p. 54, Ibid., 816.

p. 54, Ibid.

pp. 55–56, John Eaton, *Grant, Lincoln and the Freedmen: Reminiscences of the Civil War with Special Reference to the Work for the Contrabands and Freedmen of the Mississippi Valley* (New York: Longman's, Green, and Co., 1907), 79-80.

p. 56, Emmy E. Werner, *Reluctant Witnesses: Children's Voices from the Civil War* (Boulder, CO: Westview Press, 1998), 124.

p. 56, W. T. Sherman to A. Lincoln, 22 December 1864, in *War of the Rebellion: Official Records of the Union and Confederate Armies*, vol. 44 (Washington, D.C.: Government Printing Office, 1893), 783.

p. 56, William H. Runge, ed., *Four Years in the Confederate Artillery: The Diary of Private Henry Robinson Berkeley* (Richmond: Virginia Historical Society, 1991), 114.

p. 56, William C. Davis, *Jefferson Davis: The Man and His Hour* (New York: HarperCollins Publishers, 1991), 600.

p. 57, Sherman, *Memoirs of General W. T. Sherman*, 734.

p. 58, Tapert, ed., *The Brothers' War*, 232.

p. 62, Mingo White, interviewed, in *The American Slave: A Composite Autobiography*, ed. George P. Rawick, vol. 6, *Alabama and Indiana Narratives* (Westport, CT: Greenwood Publishing Co., 1972), 421.

For quoted material in sidebars:

p. 8, Bell Irvin Wiley, *The Life of Billy Yank: The Common Soldier of the Union* (Baton Rouge: Louisiana State University Press, 1978), 280.

pp. 8–9, Ibid.

p. 9, Ibid.

p. 9, Ibid., 279–280.

p. 10, Steven A. Channing, *Confederate Ordeal: The Southern Home Front* (Alexandria, VA: Time-Life Books, 1984), 88.

p. 10, Tapert, ed., *The Brothers' War*, 127–128.

p. 10, Bell Irvin Wiley, *The Life of Johnny Reb: The Common Soldier of the Confederacy* (Baton Rouge: Louisiana State University Press, 1978), 228.

p. 40, Philip Katcher, *The American Civil War Source Book* (London: Arms and Armour Press, 1992), 118.

p. 40, Ibid., 119.

p. 41, Ibid.

p. 44, McPherson, *Battle Cry of Freedom*, 776.

p. 65, Walter Calloway, interviewed, in *The American Slave: A Composite Autobiography*, ed. George P. Rawick, vol. 6, *Alabama and Indiana Narratives* (Westport, CT: Greenwood Publishing Co., 1972), 53.

p. 65, Gus Askew, interviewed, in *The American Slave: A Composite Autobiography*, ed. George P. Rawick, vol. 6, *Alabama and Indiana Narratives* (Westport, CT: Greenwood Publishing Co., 1972), 15.

p. 65, William Towns, interviewed, in *The American Slave: A Composite Autobiography*, ed. George P. Rawick, vol. 6, *Alabama and Indiana Narratives* (Westport, CT: Greenwood Publishing Co., 1972), 392.

p. 65, Mary Ella Grandberry, interviewed, in *The American Slave: A Composite Autobiography*, ed. George P. Rawick, vol. 6, *Alabama and Indiana Narratives* (Westport, CT: Greenwood Publishing Co., 1972), 163.

For quoted material in captions:

p. 5, Dale E. Floyd, ed., *"Dear Friends at Home . . . ": The Letters and Diary of Thomas James Owen, Fiftieth New York Volunteer Engineer Regiment, During the Civil War* (Washington, D.C.: Government Printing Office, 1985), 34.

p. 5, Ibid., 28.

p. 11, J. Longstreet to A. Lawton, 5 March 1864, in *War of the Rebellion: Official Records of the Union and Confederate Armies*, vol. 32, part III (Washington, D.C.: Government Printing Office, 1890), 588.

p. 12, Gary W. Gallagher, ed., *Fighting for the Confederacy: The Personal Recollections of General Edward Porter Alexander* (Chapel Hill: University of North Carolina Press, 1989), 345.

p. 21, John Gibbon, *Personal Recollections of the Civil War by John Gibbon, Brigadier-General, U.S.A.* (Dayton, OH: Morningside Bookshop) 1978), 216–217.

p. 29, Bruce Catton, *Grant Takes Command* (New York: Little, Brown & Co., 1969), 235-236.

p. 48, Tapert, ed., *The Brothers' War*, 205.

p. 50, Werner, *Reluctant Witnesses*, 113.

p. 50, Ibid.

p. 50, Runge, ed., *Four Years in the Confederate Artillery*, 95.

p. 52, Thomas Buchanan Read, "Sheridan's Ride," in *The Photographic History of the Civil War*, Francis Trevelyan Miller, vol. 9, *Poetry and Eloquence from the Blue and the Gray* (New York: Thomas Yoseloff, 1957), 70–72.

p. 55, Tapert, ed., *The Brothers' War*, 228.

Selected Bibliography

Arnold, James R. *The Armies of U. S. Grant*. London: Arms and Armour Press, 1995.

Boatner, Mark Mayo, III. *The Civil War Dictionary*. New York: David McKay Co., 1959.

Catton, Bruce. *A Stillness at Appomattox*. Garden City, NY: Doubleday & Co., 1953.

Gallagher, Gary W., ed. *The Wilderness Campaign*. Chapel Hill: University of North Carolina Press, 1997.

Grant, Ulysses S. *Personal Memoirs*. 1885. Reprint, New York: Da Capo Press, 1982.

McDonough, James Lee, and James Pickett Jones. *War So Terrible: Sherman and Atlanta*. New York: W. W. Norton & Co., 1987.

McPherson, James M. *Battle Cry of Freedom*. New York: Oxford University Press, 1988.

Rawick, George P., ed. *The American Slave: A Composite Autobiography*. 19 vols. Westport, CT: Greenwood Publishing Co., 1972.

Robertson, James I., ed. *The Civil War Letters of General Robert McAllister*. New Brunswick, NJ: Rutgers University Press, 1965.

Sherman, William T. *Memoirs of General W. T. Sherman*. New York: The Library of America, 1990.

Tapert, Annette, ed. *The Brothers' War: Civil War Letters to Their Loved Ones from the Blue and Gray*. New York: Times Books, 1988.

For More Information

Books

Brooks, Victor. *African-Americans in the Civil War*. Philadelphia: Chelsea House, 2000.

Burchard, Peter. *Lincoln and Slavery*. New York: Atheneum, 1999.

Clinton, Catherine. *Scholastic Encyclopedia of the Civil War*. New York: Scholastic, Inc., 1999.

Collier, Christopher, and James Lincoln Collier. *Reconstruction and the Rise of Jim Crow, 1864-1896*. New York: Benchmark Books, 2000.

Day, Nancy. *Your Travel Guide to Civil War America*. Minneapolis: Runestone Press, 2001.

Frazier, Joey. *Jefferson Davis*. New York: Chelsea House, 2000.

Freedman, Russell. *Lincoln: A Photobiography*. New York: Clarion Books, 1987.

Grabowski, Patricia. *Robert E. Lee*. Philadelphia: Chelsea House, 2000.

Hakim, Joy. *Reconstruction and Reform*. New York: Oxford University Press, 1994.

———. *War, Terrible War*. New York: Oxford University Press, 1994.

Marrin, Albert. *Unconditional Surrender: U. S. Grant and the Civil War*. New York: Atheneum, 1994.

Mettger, Zak. *Till Victory Is Won: Black Soldiers in the Civil War*. New York: Lodestar Books, 1994.

Ransom, Candace F. *Children of the Civil War*. Minneapolis: Carolrhoda Books, 1998.

Remstein, Henna R. *William Sherman: Union General*. Philadelphia: Chelsea House, 2001.

Stanchak, John. *Civil War*. New York: Dorling Kindersley, 2000.

Videos

Andersonville. Atlanta: Turner Network Television, 1995.

The Civil War. Walpole, NH: Florentine Films, 1990. Videocassette series. This PBS series by Ken Burns and narrated by David McCullough includes personal accounts and archival photos, as well as commentary on the period by many writers.

Web Sites

<http://www.civilwarletters.com/home.html>
Letters of an Iowa soldier in the Civil War

<http://www.nps.gov/pete/mahan/PNBhome.html>
National Park Service site for the Petersburg National Battlefield, includes an interactive page for students

<http://www.coax.net/people/lwf/data.htm>
U.S. Colored Troops in the Civil War

<http://www.cr.nps.gov/seac/andearch/html>
National Park Service site describing the archaeological dig at Andersonville Prison

Places to Visit

Appomattox Court House National Historical Park, Appomattox, Virginia: 1,325 acres, including the battlefield and reconstructed or restored town buildings

Fredericksburg and Spotsylvania National Military Park, Fredericksburg, Virginia: includes Fredericksburg, Chancellorsville, the Wilderness, and Spotsylvania Court House Battlefields, each of them more than one thousand acres

Petersburg National Battlefield, Petersburg, Virginia: about 2,700 acres: includes original earthworks, the Crater, City Point (the Union supply depot), and Five Forks Battlefield

Ford's Theatre National Historic Site, Washington, D.C.: the place where Abraham Lincoln was shot, restored to look like it did at the time

Index

>─┤◄►─●─◄├─◄

About the Authors

James R. Arnold was born in Illinois, and his family moved to Switzerland when he was a teenager. His fascination with the history of war was born on the battlefields of Europe. He returned to the United States for his college education. For the past twenty-five years, he and his wife, Roberta Wiener, have lived and farmed in the Shenandoah Valley of Virginia and toured all the Civil War battlefields.

Mr. Arnold's great-great-grandfather was shot and killed in Fairfax, Virginia, because he voted against secession. Another ancestor served in an Ohio regiment during the Civil War. Mr. Arnold has written more than twenty books about American and European wars, and he has contributed to many others.

Roberta Wiener grew up in Pennsylvania and completed her education in Washington, D.C. After many years of touring battlefields and researching books with her husband, James R. Arnold, she has said, "The more I learn about war, the more fascinating it becomes." Ms. Wiener has coauthored nine books with Mr. Arnold and edited numerous educational books, including a children's encyclopedia. She has also worked as an archivist for the U.S. Army.

Picture Acknowledgments

Appomattox National Historical Park/photo by Robert Pankey: front cover. *Frank Leslie's Illustrated Newspaper:* 55. Library of Congress: 8–9, 16–17, 23, 26–27, 28, 30–31, 32–33, 46, 47, 48–49, 50–51, 54, 59, 62–63. National Archives: 6–7, 11, 12, 13, 14–15, 23–24, 24, 29, 32, 38–39, 43, 45, 51, 52, 56–57. National Guard Bureau: 59. National Park Service: 14, 18. South Carolina Library, University of South Carolina: Back cover. U.S. Army Military History Institute: 36–37. Virginia Military Institute: 34–35. West Point Museum Collection, U.S. Military Academy: 5, 41, 60. Robert W. Wilson, Woodruff, SC: Title page.

West Point Museum Collection photography by Anthony Mairo
Maps by Jerry Malone